FamilyCircle
Easy
wreaths

FamilyCircle

Easy wreaths

50 IDEAS
FOR EVERY SEASON

sixth&spring
books

Sixth&Spring Books
233 Spring Street
New York, NY 10013

Editorial Director
Trisha Malcolm

Art Director
Christy Hale

Cover Design
Chi Ling Moy

Book Division Manager
Erica Smith

Production Manager
David Joinnides

President and Publisher, Sixth&Spring Books
Art Joinnides

Family Circle Magazine

Senior Editor
Jonna Gallo

Consulting Editor
Barbara Winkler

Library of Congress Catalog-in-Publication Data
Library of Congress Control Number: 2005926332
ISBN 1-931543-80-1
ISBN-13: 978-1-931543-80-4

1 3 5 7 9 10 8 6 4 2

Manufactured in China

Contents

INTRODUCTION

"There ought to be gardens for all months in the year, in which, severally, things of beauty may be in season." —Sir Francis Bacon

Would that Mother Nature would heed the English statesman and philosopher. But even without Her full cooperation, every part of the year brings forth flowers, foliage and other elements perfect for creating a harbinger of welcome unlike any other: a wreath. Spring and summer bring flower choices so copious, so over-the-top glorious, that choosing is almost a burden; think roses, hydrangeas, petunias, daffodils, daisies galore. But fall and winter also arrive bearing gifts, from fiery foliage and fragrant evergreens to plump pinecones and cheery red berries. Really, almost anything that strikes your fancy can be tucked into or twisted around a form of one sort or another to produce a wreath. The possibilities are vast, and the satisfaction of making something with your own two hands is tremendous. And as if that were not sufficient motivation, somehow, a wreath serves as an invitation to passers-by that they have come upon a place of comfort and warmth.

A BRIEF HISTORY LESSON

*W*hat we commonly know today as a wreath harkens back many centuries. Wreaths descend from fabric headbands called diadems in the Persian Empire, derived from the old Greek word *diadema*, which literally means "thing bound around." The Greeks fashioned laurel leaves into head garlands to bestow upon victors in the Olympic Games. Ancient brides almost always put wreaths on their heads; the unbroken circles were viewed as symbols of purity. In ancient Rome, brides and grooms alike wore circles fashioned of grain, symbolizing hoped-for fertility; the general citizenry also displayed wreaths as symbols of victory and celebration. Fast-forward to the 15th century, and ordinary members of the working class began wearing circlets on their heads for religious holidays. How wreaths moved from heads to doors, where they commonly hang today, is not certain, but conventional wisdom holds that people were so enamored of their headpieces that rather than discard them, they placed them on the wall or door. Over time, this evolved into the beloved tradition of adorning one's home with a seasonal display.

GETTING STARTED

*O*f course, if you choose to purchase a wreath, home stores and catalogs abound with lovely options. But if you are reading this book, chances are you would rather create something on your own. Happily, making a wreath is an eminently doable, not to mention delightful, project. It needn't be terribly time-consuming or expensive. (For a list of resources, turn to page 124.) And there are few hard-and-fast rules. Let our photos and how-to's guide you. But more importantly, follow wherever your heart leads. Always decide at the outset where the hanger will go, because that choice orients you, the artist, as to top and bottom. It also determines the focus of the finished wreath. Play for a time with placement of flowers, leaves, or whatever you're using, then step back and look over your work from a variety of angles and vantage points. Feel free to move things about a bit, or a lot, or even to start over again. You may even wish to position the wreath before it is completely finished, since it will look different hanging vertically than it does laying flat. It's up to you. Both the creative process and end result are yours and yours alone.

BASES TO BUILD UPON

*A*s with anything else, the foundation you choose for a wreath makes a big difference, in terms of both workability and the finished result. Here are the most commonly used wreath forms, shown in the photo below. If you come upon a good sale, stock up so you can craft whenever the mood strikes.

- Floral foam (also sometimes called oasis). Invented for use with fresh flowers, it must be immersed in water until saturated before you insert plant materials.
- Plastic foam. Best for dried arrangements and light elements.
- Moss-coated foam. Good for dried materials when some of the background will remain visible.
- Grapevine. Great for dried or fresh wreaths; weathers well and adds a natural, easygoing air.
- Wire box frame (not shown). Comprised of two or more concentric wire circles with spacers in between.
- Straw (also not shown.) Versatile, sturdy and densely packed; holds florist's pins well.

TOOLS OF THE TRADE

*B*esides an appropriate wreath base, you'll need a few other aids on hand (beyond the flowers and leaves) so you can work easily and uninterrupted. Each wreath has how-to's specifying what is required, but the list that follows is a good general guideline. You're likely to have many of the items in your household already. If not, any well-stocked craft or hobby shop or nursery will stock them.

- High- and low-temperature glue guns, plus appropriate glue sticks, for affixing dry elements
- Stem stripper, for removing leaves and thorns from roses
- Florist's wire of various gauges, on spools or in pre-cut lengths, to attach components of various weights; florist's pins, not shown, are another option
- Wire cutter
- Sharp scissors

Not pictured, but smart to keep in stock:
- Plastic floral vials to fill with water (for individual blooms)
- Flexible measuring tape
- Small pair of pliers
- Tweezers
- Tacky glue

LAST WORDS OF ADVICE

To give fresh wreaths a head start:
- Add a little bleach and sugar to the water in which you soak the florist foam, to fight bacteria and nourish flowers.
- Trim flowers of unwanted foliage, recut stems, and soak in water in a cool place for at least 6 hours prior to using.
- As blooms wilt, spritz lightly with water.

In terms of placement:
- Whenever possible, site wreaths out of direct contact with sunlight or rain.
- If keeping wreath indoors, avoid a spot too near a radiator or heating vent.

If you need to transport your masterpiece:
- Find a box large enough to accommodate the wreath lying flat. Line the bottom with white tissue paper, lay in wreath, then gently but firmly stuff corners with wadded white tissue to prevent any movement.
- If your wreath does not have a flat back, hang by its hanger on the hook on either side of your car's back seat.

FALL

"Autumn is a
second spring when
every leaf is a flower," said
French philosopher Albert Camus.
These unique ideas speak
to the specialness
of this time of
year.

This stunner pointedly ignores the notion that a proper wreath must be round; a rectangular base provides a fetching, modern framework for wheat and berries.

Four Corners

You need:

straight twigs (available at floral suppliers); saw or pruning shears; raffia; sprays of wheat and berries; hot glue gun and glue sticks; nuts; dried leaves

To do:

To create base, cut 10 to 15 twigs, each 20 inches long, for side pieces. Cut the same number of twigs, each 18 inches long, for top and bottom pieces. Divide groups in half and make two bundles of equal diameter from both lengths. On work surface, position 2 20-inch bundles parallel to each other, about 14 inches apart. Position shorter lengths crosswise across top and bottom, about 16 inches apart. Twigs should extend past corners where bundles cross about 2 inches. Use raffia to lash bundles together at corners. Tie ends of raffia into a tight knot to secure. Arrange wheat and berry sprays to radiate from corners; glue in place. Overlap and fill in spaces with shorter and longer sprays, tucking ends between twigs and securing with glue. Arrange leaves and nuts in corners; glue in place. Fill spaces with smaller or shorter elements. Allow some twigs and raffia ties to show.

*O*ak leaves cradle a combination of elements
that evoke the spirit of the outdoors on the cusp of frost.

Pinecone Panoply

You need:

grapevine wreath; oak leaves; sweet gum seedpods; pinecones; bittersweet berries; crab apples; hot-glue gun and glue sticks; hair spray (optional)

To do:

Fill out grapevine form with oak leaves by tucking stems into nooks and crannies. Tuck berries among the leaves. Glue on seed pods and other materials. For extra hold, spritz finished wreath with hair spray.

As flowers start to wane and leaves begin to fall, cheer up the garden with the crimson glory of a rustic cranberry wreath. This is so easy to make, you could turn out several and perch them on small twiggy stands or suspend them from tree branches to sway in the breeze.

Berry Delight

You need:

heart-shaped grapevine wreath; fresh cranberries; florist's wire; length of grapevine; three small twigs

To do:

String cranberries on wire until you have a length long enough to wrap around wreath. (To make the stringing easier, you could use a few smaller strips of wire for stringing, then attach together for desired measurement.) Drape the cranberry garland over wreath, tucking ends of wire into wreath to secure. Fold extra length of grapevine in two and twist together; attach to wreath near top with florist's wire to form an extra perch for birds. (Optional: To make stand, simply wire three small twigs together. Set wreath atop stand by wiring into place.)

A palette of warm, earthy browns
seems to suit the season, while pheasant feathers
tucked here and there add an air of sophistication.

Feathery Feat

You need:

twig wreath; tallow berries; pinecones; copper eucalyptus and skeleton leaves; pheasant feathers; ribbon; hot-glue gun and glue sticks

To do:

Hot-glue tallow berries, pinecones and eucalyptus randomly around wreath. Roll skeleton leaves into cone shapes, pinching small ends and securing with dabs of glue. Affix to wreath with more glue, placing where desired. Trim feathers to appropriate length; tuck in and glue. Tie on ribbon bow to finish.

$\mathcal{B}$erries, leaves, nuts, a crisp fall apple
as the focal point: This wreath brims with
a feeling of wonderful abundance that
will entice all who pass by.

Autumn Splendor

You need:

plastic foam wreath form; rust-colored, 3-inch-wide grosgrain ribbon; florist's pins; apple; fresh or fried seasonal leaves such as oak, magnolia and seeded eucalyptus; acorns; berries such as bittersweet, viburnum, pepperberries and St. John's wort; ornamental grasses such as wheat; dried flowers such as safflower; mimosa and billy buttons; seedheads of black-eyed Susan; clippers; hot-glue gun and glue stick; florist's pins; knife; large nail; floral wire

To do:

Wrap ribbon around wreath form, overlapping edges to cover completely; secure in place with pins. Decide on anchor point of wreath and mark; this is where the apple will be placed and will be the focus of the finished project. Working around the circle from anchor point, glue or pin leaves into place. Apply additional items in layers, varying colors and shapes and building up to desired effect; stick just tips of stems into wreath to maintain three-dimensional quality. When desired fullness is reached, place apple at anchor point, securing in place with nail. (You may wish to cut away a small part of the back of the apple so you can attach it to the wreath more easily.) Cut a length of wire; fold in half and twist ends together to form a hanger; push ends into back of wreath at top center.

*G*ilded orange peels,
raffia-tied cinnamon sticks and nutmeg nuggets mingle
in an aromatic wreath that will perfume the
air to your nose's content.

Spice Scent-sation

You need:

12-inch grapevine wreath; cinnamon sticks, dried oranges; raffia; gilt wax; dried mace; pieces of whole nutmeg; hazelnuts; hot-glue gun and glue sticks; florist's wire

To do:

Arrange cinnamon sticks into 6 equal bundles; tie with raffia. Rub cinnamon bundles and oranges with gilt wax and sprinkle mace over oranges. (It will stick to the wax.) Glue on cinnamon bundles at approximately even intervals all around, then glue on oranges, nutmeg cloves and hazelnuts. Fold wire in half; twist to form hanging loop. Twist ends around back of wreath at top center.

*E*veryone knows birds love berries, so why not treat our fine-feathered friends to a high-flying feeder that's decorative as well as delicious.

For the Birds

You need:

grapevine wreath; lots of small twigs; 3 lengths of twine, each 36-inches long; clusters of berries, such as currants or winterberries; small sprigs of leaves

To do:

Fill in grapevine wreath with small twigs to make it denser and fuller. Tuck in sprays of berries all around wreath; add leaf sprigs for a lush effect. Mark off three equidistant points on wreath and loop lengths of twine around wreath at these points, knotting each length together at end. Hold pieces of twine together tautly above wreath and knot all three lengths together around a D-ring. Make any adjustments necessary to assure that wreath hangs evenly from the D-ring. Attach to branch or bracket so birds can perch on wreath and peck at the berries.

*O*ranges, yellows, reds, and rust—
all the brilliant hues of autumn—come
together in a celebratory circle of color,
just right for your front door.

Fall on Fire

You need:

grapevine wreath; Japanese lanterns; straw flowers; hypericum berries; orange wire-edged ribbon; florist's wire

To do:

Tuck ingedients into crevices of grapevine wreath, working in layers and adding additional elements until desired lushness is achieved. Tie ribbon into a bow; wire to top of wreath. Affix a straw flower to the center of the bow with a length of wire.

$\mathcal{H}$alloween is the perfect time to show your spirit! This round, replete with slithery spiders and wispy ghouls, is at once creepy and charming.

Ghostly Circle

You need:

off-white silk fabric; 1- and 2-inch diameter plastic foam balls; fabric stiffener; thread and needle; permanent marker; grapevine wreath; skeleton bodhi leaves; Chinese lantern pods; bittersweet berry branches; dried lychees; tacky glue; florist's wire; orange sheer and satin ribbons; plastic spiders

To do:

To make ghosts, cut 14" squares of silk fabric for large ones and 7" squares for small ones. In a bowl, stir together equal parts fabric stiffener and water; dip fabric pieces in mixture. Wrap larger pieces around larger balls and smaller pieces around smaller balls, draping and folding fabric as desired. Sew a long thread at the top of each to use as hanger, then hang so ghosts keep shape until completely dry. Remove thread. Trim fabric edges as needed. Use permanent marker to draw on faces. To make wreath, arrange skeleton leaves, Chinese lanterns, lychees and bittersweet berry branches around wreath as desired and glue or wire in place. Glue fabric ghosts around wreath. Drape lengths of sheer ribbon gracefully around wreath, gluing here and there to keep in place. Holding lengths of satin and sheer ribbon together, tie into a bow. Glue bow onto wreath. Glue spiders onto bow and onto a few ghosts.

HOLIDAY

"Happy,
happy Christmas that
can transport the traveler back
to his own fireside and quiet home,"
noted Charles Dickens. These
decorations all offer
the comfort of
the season.

*W*reaths decorated with fruits have long been a symbol of hospitality and welcome, and this one is particularly grand. With its scintillating colors and sumptuous textures, this creation is a glorious homage to nature's generosity.

Gifts of Nature

You need:

leafy wreath (magnolia, laurel, salal or smilax); assorted dried produce: lemons, limes, oranges, pomegranates, artichokes (available in crafts stores); florist's wire; hot glue gun and glue sticks; small sprays of wheat; faux berry garland

To do:

With florist's wire or glue, affix the produce to the wreath in a pleasing pattern. A good rule of thumb is to group like ingredients together (use photo as a guide) in clusters around the wreath. With florist's wire, attach sprays of wheat here and there. Finish up by twining the berry garland around the wreath, affixing with wire to keep in place.

You can't get more traditional than a red, green and white color scheme, but everything else about this lush candle display is totally cutting edge.

Garden of Eden

You need:

sturdy cardboard; scissors; pencil; ruler; craft knife; aluminum foil; floral foam; electrical tape; red carnations; red-and-white-striped carnations; boxwood; glass hurricane to fit in center; white candle

To do:

To fashion a base, cut a 12-inch cardboard square. Using a ruler as your guide, draw a square in the center, 3 inches from edge all around; cut out smaller square with craft knife. Wrap large square with aluminum foil. Cut floral foam to fit on top; attach with electrical tape. Immerse in water until well-saturated. Cut carnation stems short. Insert a row of striped flowers at inner edge, then red ones. Edge with boxwood. Position hurricane in center, then add candle.

atiny Christmas balls are suited for more than gracing the boughs of your tree, as this opulent display affirms. Go for the gusto with a wreath that will last for generations if you pack it away carefully each year.

Having a Ball

You need:

18-inch plastic foam wreath form; 2-inch-wide ribbon in color that coordinates with ornaments; hot-glue gun and glue sticks; large, medium and small ornaments; pencil; florist's pins; bow

To do:

Cover inner edge of wreath form with ribbon; hot-glue or pin to secure in place. With pointed end of a pencil, poke about a dozen holes all around the wreath. Insert stem end of largest balls into these holes. When pleased with placement, hot-glue into position. Repeat with medium and small balls until form is covered. Now build a second layer of medium and small balls, applying hot glue around stem and sticking between balls on first layer. Continue until form is covered. Camouflage outside edge of form with more ribbon; hot-glue or pin into place. Finish with a bow.

Combine preppy plaid with
a passel of perky pups and you get
a wreath sure to win everyone over.
Blanket-stitching on the pooches
adds a homespun note.

Puttin' On the Dog

You need:

Scottie dog cookie cutter; black felt; red embroidery thread; embroidery needle; fiberfill stuffing; narrow plaid ribbon; small jingle bells; hot-glue gun and glue sticks or tacky glue; plastic foam wreath form; 2"-wide plaid ribbon; sprigs of boxwood and ferns; contrasting solid ribbon

To do:

To sew Scottie dogs, fold felt in half. Using cookie cutter as a template, cut through both layers to cut out front and back pieces. Repeat to cut out fronts and backs for 7 or 8 dogs. Holding wrong sides together, use red embroidery thread and work blanket stitch around dog shapes, leaving an opening for stuffing. Stuff lightly; blanket-stitch opening closed. Thread a jingle bell on lengths of narrow ribbon; tie ribbons into bows around dog necks. Glue one end of wide ribbon on wrong side of wreath form, then wrap all around form, overlapping edges to cover completely; glue other end in place, also on wrong side. Glue dogs around wreath. Tuck sprigs of boxwood and ferns under ribbon edges. Wrap contrasting ribbon around top of wreath; tie ends into a bow for hanging.

So airy and delicate it looks as if it might melt in the sun, this ethereal ring is actually quite durable. The sparkle and shine mimic the icy flakes you find in the stillness after a snowstorm.

Silver Lace

You need:

grapevine wreath; matte silver spray paint; faux silver berries; faux sage leaves; wide satin chartreuse ribbon

To do:

Spray-paint entire wreath silver; let dry completely. Twine faux berries all around, then tuck in clusters of faux sage leaves here and there. To hang, suspend from a wide satin chartreuse ribbon.

An assortment of kitten-sized mittens turns a basic evergreen circle into one that's certain to elicit compliments for craftiness and creativity.

Hands-Down Favorite

You need:

evergreen wreath; mitten-shaped cookie cutter, cardboard; red and white felt; pinking shears; sewing machine and thread; holiday-motif fabric; gold trim; tacky glue; fiberfill stuffing; miniature gold star patches; narrow red ribbon; shiny wide gold ribbon; small ornaments; florist's wire

To do:

To fashion a mitten template, trace a cookie cutter (or just draw freehand) on cardboard and cut out. Trace onto red and white felt, allowing two shapes per mitten for front and back; cut out using pinking shears. Sew matching pieces together, about ¼" in from edge, leaving wrist ends open. Layer strips of holiday-motif fabric and fancy gold trim across edges; glue in place. Lightly stuff mittens with fiberfill; stitch shut. On each, glue a gold star on front center and a piece of narrow red ribbon at back; use latter to tie mittens to wreath. Wind gold ribbon all around as shown, then wire on assorted small ornaments to finish.

*I*n this twist on the traditional, there's nary a touch of green. Instead, think tightly packed silver and white balls for a gleaming, glamorous presentation. Position anyplace the orbs can reflect light for a spectacular show.

Snow Day

You need:

plastic foam wreath form; rolled cotton; string; white and silver glass ball ornaments in two sizes; low-temp glue gun and glue sticks; white faux leaf and beaded berry branches

To do:

Wrap wreath form with rolled cotton to cover completely and secure with a length of string. Remove wire hangers from all balls. (If possible, bend hanger wire straight, replace on ball and poke wire into foam before gluing.) Arrange a row of larger ornaments around center of wreath and glue into place. Arrange and secure a row of small white ornaments along each side of large ones. Continue to glue on rows of silver and white smaller ornaments until wreath has been filled, including the inner rim. (Leave back flat so you can hang wreath easily.) Position faux branches at top edge and poke into foam; secure with glue if necessary.

For a sensational—not to mention scented—conversation piece, look no further than an evergreen wreath rotated on the horizontal. Add twinkling white lights and sparkly dangles and you have a breathtaking display.

Chandelier Chic

You need:

evergreen wreath; gauzy ribbon; battery-powered miniature white lights; florist's wire; glass or acrylic snowflake ornaments; various clear baubles

To do:

Tie a long length of ribbon at each of four evenly spaced points around wreath. Weave battery-powered lights in and around wreath, securing with wire as necessary. Add ornaments as desired. Pull ribbons together at top into a big bow and hang.

Graceful musical notes, a glitzy gold instrument: This unusual round evokes the sounds of the season. The mere sight of it will set you to humming your favorite carols in no time.

It's In the Stars

You need:

plastic foam wreath form; musical paper; white glue; mixing bucket; paint brush; gold cording; hot-glue gun and glue sticks; gold star ornaments, plain and glittered; gold instrument ornament; wide gold sheer ribbon

To do:

In bucket, mix equal parts glue and water. Rip musical paper into strips, each about 4" or 5" wide. Paint the back of each strip with thinned glue and wrap around foam wreath. Continue to add strips, overlapping and changing directions until wreath is completely covered. Use gold cord to suspend a single star from top center of wreath so it hangs freely in center. Arrange remaining star ornaments all over wreath, gluing in place. Add a single gold instrument on side of wreath. Tie a length of ribbon around top of wreath, with a big bow for a hanger.

*T*hinking beyond a door or wall as a backdrop led to this utterly charming vignette. Muse on how you could freeze such a moment in your home—all you need is the wreath; the rest is up to you.

Best Seat In the House

You need:

small evergreen wreath; red wire-edged ribbon; florist's wire; child-size chair; teddy bears; vintage book

To do:

Tie red ribbon into a bow and wire to wreath. Wire wreath to top of the chair. On seat, set a pair of teddies, a yesteryear children's book, anything you like.

A total absence of greenery and pine-y aroma doesn't mean this creative display isn't brimming with Christmas spirit. Hang with pride any place that could use sparkle to spare.

Beaded Baubles

You need:

Two same-size beaded garlands; florist's wire; glass ornament in coordinating color; coordinating ribbon

To do:

Bend each garland into a circle form, then place one circle inside other in a perpendicular fashion as shown. Secure with florist's wire top and bottom to keep in place. With florist's wire, suspend ornament from top intersection to swing freely in center. Tie on a vivid bow and hang.

Red-and-white checks are packed with old-fashioned country charm. No matter how long your December to-do list, this will fill you with good cheer.

Homespun Holiday

You need:

plastic foam wreath form; various wired-edged red-and-white-check ribbons; hot-glue gun and glue sticks

To do:

Decide which ribbon you wish to use as the base. Glue one end to wrong side of wreath form; wrap ribbon continuously around form, overlapping edges to cover completely. Glue other end to wrong side of wreath. Tie ribbon segments into bows; glue all over wreath.

*A*nywhere, any time, creamy white roses bespeak class. Wire them to a lush green wreath and you have an awesome addition to a wall or door.

Coming Up Roses

You need:

boxwood wreath; white roses; floral vials; white ball ornaments; other white or silver ornaments if desired

To do:

Cut rose stems short and insert each into a water-filled floral vial. Wind wire around tops of vials and affix to boxwood, spacing as desired. Wire on additional ornaments. Mist thoroughly with water.

For a party, consider mini-wreaths as chairback décor. Invite guests to take theirs home as a memento.

Heart on a String

You need:

small grapevine wreaths; faux berry vine; plaid fabric; needle and thread; fiberfill stuffing; red sequin trim; thin gold cord; sheer red ribbon

To do:

Wind faux berry vine around wreath form. To make center adornment, cut two hearts out of plaid fabric. Stitch, wrong sides together, leaving an opening for turning and stuffing. Turn right-side-out; lightly fill; stitch closed. Sew on sequin trim in heart shape as shown. Stitch a loop of gold cording to center top of heart and tie around top of wreath so heart dangles freely in center. Repeat for additional mini-wreaths. Attach wreaths to backs of chairs with sheer red ribbon.

WINTER

According to
an ancient Japanese
proverb, one kind word can
warm three winter months. So can
any of these heartwarming,
handmade cold-weather
displays.

Guests can't help but smile when they are welcomed by this scarf-clad greeter. Happily, there are no melting woes if the sun makes an appearance.

Snowman Sentinel

You need:

three evergreen wreaths in graduated sizes; florist's wire; thrift-store hat that you are willing to cut in half; scissors; scarf

To do:

Gently lay wreaths back side down on floor, smallest to largest. Attach securely one to another with florist's wire; turn over. Tie scarf around the bottom of smallest wreath. Cut hat in half neatly; wire to top of smallest wreath. (You will need to cut a few slashes in hat so you can pass wire through to attach.)

*A*ll the greens sashaying 'round make this verdant visage the equivalent of a wintertime walk in the forest. But this can be enjoyed from indoors; no bundling up required.

Ever Green

You need:

metal wreath form; sufficient sphagnum moss to fill; plastic wrap; pruners; assorted winter greens such as white pine, spruce, hemlock and cedar; assorted seasonal berry branches, such as holly, with variegated and solid leaves

To do:

Dampen sphagnum moss and stuff gently into frame. Wrap entire form with plastic wrap to hold in moisture. Cut evergeen branches on diagonal with pruners and poke through plastic into sphagnum moss. When satisfied with lushness, cut berry branches on diagonal and insert.

The square shape is like a window onto Mother Nature's nonstop show. The cardinal in the corner serves as a sweet reminder that even in the bleakest season, birds will sing.

Natural Wonder

You need:

square wire wreath base; sufficient sphagnum moss to fill; plastic wrap; sprigs of rose hips; faux cardinal; florist's wire

To do:

Thoroughly dampen moss, then pack into wreath base. Wrap entire form with plastic wrap to hold in moisture. Insert sprigs of rose hips in a random pattern, letting branches fall as they may. Wire a cardinal onto the corner.

This round resounds with a splendid symphony of reds, yellows, oranges and greens. Be generous with the add-ons for a stunning statement.

Fanciful Fruits

You need:

plastic foam wreath form; faux berries in reds, purples and greens; small faux fruits such as apples, pears, pomegranates, lemons, limes and oranges; assorted artificial leaves, branches and twigs in varying shapes and colors; florist's pins; low-temp glue gun and glue sticks

To do:

Start at one spot on foam wreath and, working in one direction, insert berries, fruits and leaves around front and sides of wreath until satisfied with appearance. Overlap elements by tucking branches and twigs under smaller ingredients. Fill in any remaining nooks and crannies with small leaves, affixing with glue or florist's pins as warranted.

Inspired by an old English folk song, this quick-to-do project melds the sculpture of a topiary with the lushness of a potted plant for a truly dynamic display. This wreath takes the edge off the cold by warming the heart.

You need:

variegated ivy plant in pretty cachepot (or basket); grapevine wreath; more ivy for wrapping grapevine; scissors; florist's pins; holly branches; ribbon

To do:

Cut long snippets of ivy and wrap artfully around grapevine wreath, tucking ends into crevices. When satisfied with level of lushness, position wreath atop potted plant and secure in place with pins as needed. Nestle holly at base. Tie bow at top and let ends of ribbon stream down around topiary. Mist ivy and holly regularly to keep fresh.

imple, humble, rustic...
this display of ruby-colored berries
lends any setting a just-right touch
of Americana.

Star Bright

You need:
two lengths of sturdy wire, one slightly longer than the other; fresh cranberries; florist's wire; raffia

To do:
Thread cranberries on both lengths of wire. Lay wires side by side on work surface, then bend both into a star shape. At each star point, connect wire pieces with florist's wire. Wrap raffia between cranberries to bind everything together.

A wispy, uncontrived wreath like this captures the essence of the great outdoors; it's tempting to wait for an optimistic flyer to come perch.

Bird Call

You need:

grapevine wreath; dried flowers such as hydrangeas, sunflower heads and yarrow; pinecones; winterberries; dried wisteria; purchased bird's nest; dried wheat acorns or nuts; florist's pins; pruners

To do:

Trim stems of dried flowers as necessary and insert all around wreath, taking care to vary placement and leave space around blossoms for an airy feel. Trim berry branches and insert. Bend wisteria into a loose circle; tuck ends into lower half of wreath. With florist's pins, secure bird nest to bottom and fill with acorns or nuts.

*I*nstead of being obscured as usual, the grapevine circle at the center of things shows through this arrangement for a carefree look that's somehow both polished and rough-around-the-edge.

Casual Cheer

You need:

grapevine wreath; evergreen branches; faux berries; paperwhites; floral vials; three different ribbons: gingham, plaid and solid

To do:

Tuck evergreen branches into both front and back of wreath, allowing wreath form to remain visible at certain points. Insert faux berries around bottom half of wreath, placing in a pleasing fashion. Trim paperwhites as needed; tuck into water-filled vials. Insert vials into wreath base. Finish with a gingham bow plus streamers of plaid and solid ribbon at top right corner.

SPRING

To paraphrase
Henry Wadsworth Longfellow,
what wonder there would be in our hearts
if spring came once a century
instead of once a year.
Celebrate the season
of rebirth.

*W*hether it was a moderate or monster winter matters not; this cocky display of bold anemones, positioned within an empty frame, fuels the optimism that crops up when spring arrives.

Picture Perfect

You need:

grapevine wreath; floral vials; assorted anemones, jasmine, lily-of-the-valley; silk ribbon; empty frame

To do:

Trim flower stems and tuck each into a water-filled floral vial. Poke in all around grapevine wreath as desired. Wrap ribbon over top of wreath and frame; tie into a bow. Attach frame to wall.

The Easter bunny himself would be delighted by this door decoration! Flower-strewn eggs and winsome blooms dance around a leafy circle.

Easter Elation

You need:

hollowed eggshells (see below for instructions); plastic foam wreath form; acrylic paints in off-white and gold; paintbrushes; pressed flowers; spray adhesive; tweezers; hot-glue gun and sticks; primroses; miniature lemon, lime or orange branches; floral vials; florist's wire; baby's breath; evergreen sprigs; ribbon

To do:

Paint eggshells off-white or gold; let dry. Spray wrong sides of pressed flowers with adhesive. With tweezers, position flowers on eggs and smooth in place gently. Arrange eggs around wreath; hot-glue in place. Trim fresh flowers and fruit branches as needed, then place in water-filled floral vials. Wrap wire around top of vials, leaving extra length at ends. Position vials around wreath, pressing wire into foam. Arrange leaves to cover. Fill in as needed with baby's breath and evergreen sprigs. Tie ribbon around wreath to function as a hanger.

To empty eggs:

Rinse eggs with warm water. With needle, prick small hole in small end and a slightly larger hole in large end, inserting tip sufficiently to completely break shell membrane and yolk. Blow into small end, expelling contents into a bowl. Let dry before proceeding.

Mother Nature would be pleased at this testament to her magic: graceful paper butterflies alight among flowers both faux and real, for a beguiling showcase that's sure to charm.

Paper Fantasy

You need:

grapevine wreath; assorted paper flowers and butterflies in white, yellow, pink and purple; florist's wire; fresh waxflowers and greenery; grosgrain ribbon

To do:

Secure paper flowers and butterflies all over wreath form, inserting stems (if they have them) into crevices, or using florist's wire. Fill remaining spaces as desired by tucking in fresh flowers and leaves. When satisfied with the lushness, top with a grosgrain ribbon bow.

For a flower lover, this home-sweet-home threesome simply can't be beat. Go ahead and signal your high spirits to the world by hanging the wreaths singly or together.

Three's the Charm

♥ You need:

wire cutters; wire or wire hanger; grapevine; fresh botanicals such as ivy or other twining plant (we used smilax); small roses, including tiny sweetheart roses; florist's wire; hot-glue gun and glue sticks; ribbon

To do:

Cut wire and bend into heart shape. Wrap with grapevine, securing as needed with florist's wire. Hot-glue ivy to grapevine. Tuck in roses, securing with florist's wire and hot glue, if needed. Slip ribbon through top two corners of heart to act as hanger.

■ You need:

twigs (bundles available from floral suppliers); twine; fresh botanicals such as boxwood, johnny-jump-ups, violets or other small violas and grape hyacinth; florist's wire; hot-glue gun and glue sticks

To do:

Make four same-size bundles of twigs. Arrange bundles to form a square, ends of twigs crossing at corners. With twine, wrap and tie, lashing corners together. Trim excess. Gather small bunches of boxwood; wrap stems with florist's wire; hot-glue to wreath. Tuck blooms into boxwood; secure with florist's wire and hot glue if needed.

● You need:

grapevine; florist's wire; fresh botanicals such as laurel leaves, heather and tulips; hot-glue gun and glue sticks

To do:

Form grapevine into a circle, twisting and wrapping to desired thickness; secure with florist's wire. Gather small bunches of laurel leaves. Wrap stems with florist's wire; hot-glue to wreath. Tuck in blooms; secure with florist's wire and hot-glue if needed.

If you wish to display as a unit, as shown in the photo, very gently position wreaths in a vertical row, face-down, on work surface lined with a soft towel. (Heart should be at top.) With florist's wire, attach securely where they touch. When finished, carefully turn unit right-side-up. Hang with ribbon.

Light up the warmer months with an explosion of fresh blossoms. In a clever twist, this harbinger of brighter days starts with a picture frame instead of a wreath form.

Posie Promenade

You need:

wooden picture frame; chicken wire; wire cutters; staple gun and staples; seasonal flowers such as St. John's wort, double petunia, lace cap hydrangea, ageratum, brodiaea, thalictrum, heliotrope and coreopsis

To do:

Using wire cutters, trim chicken wire to suitable dimension for wrapping snugly around picture frame. Staple into place. Cut flower stems short; weave into wire as desired. Mist with water.

*W*hat's that age-old expression about wearing your heart on your sleeve? Happy feelings are never more clear than when you set this charmer on a fence.

Show Some Heart

You need:

heart-shaped grapevine wreath; blue cornflowers; chamomile; florist's wire; pruners

To do:

Trim flower stems, then gently push into wreath. Add leaves as desired to fill. Mist with water.

*I*n this case, the name says it all; this exuberant beauty, with its bevy of blooms, is a joyful tribute to a season that just bursts with life.

Spring Fling

You need:

floral foam wreath form; 22-gauge wire; wire cutters; florist's tape; clippers, wire-edged ribbon, florist's picks; seasonal flowers such as daffodils, narcissus, hydrangea, salal leaves

To do:

Soak floral foam until thoroughly damp. Cut a length of wire. Fold in half and then in half again. Stick ends through wreath base at back, twist together and secure with florist's tape to create a hanger. Cut flower stems and foliage branches into lengths from 4 to 6 inches. Insert stems into wreath base. Continue adding flowers and leaves to cover wreath completely. Frame outer edges with additional leaves. Mist lightly with water. Tie ribbon into a bow; position at top of wreath and secure in place with florist's picks; artfully bend long ends to follow curve of wreath.

*R*oses can be dainty and demure or luscious and luxe, and our rosy duo shows off this beloved bloom's different personalities. Pick your favorite or make both and pair together for a striking display.

Two for the Rose

◆ DIAMOND WREATH

You need:

12 dowels, about 12 inches long; white spray paint; white raffia or cord; twigs; ivy; roses; floral vials

To do:

Spray paint dowels white; let dry. Place 3 dowels alongside each other and bind together with cord about 1½ inches from top, and then again, 1½ inches from bottom. (If dowels slide under one another a bit, that's fine.) Repeat with other dowels so you have 4 bunches. Place bunches on top of one another to form a diamond shape, and lash adjacent bunches to each other, directly over previous cord. Stick twigs in between the dowels to give a more rustic look, then twine ivy vines amid the dowels. Trim roses short and put in water-filled floral vials; tuck vials between dowels at top and bottom corners of diamond.

Two for the Rose

● ROUND WREATH

You need:

floral foam wreath; ivy; assorted roses in pink, yellow, white, rose (some still in bud stage)

To do:

Soak floral foam until thoroughly damp. Cut roses so stems are short and insert stems into foam form. For best effect, arrange in clusters by color. When pleased with arrangement, fill in with ivy vines. Wrap ribbon around top of wreath and tie into a bow.

*T*his special still life gives viewers a welcome
spring sight: a bird's nest tenderly cradling
eggs. True, the nest and its contents are
faux, but the sentiment is real.

Nesting Instinct

You need:

grapevine wreath; assorted greens such as ferns, smilax and skimmia; paperwhite narcissus; florist's vials; faux bird's nest; faux quail eggs; tacky glue; florist's pins

To do:

Tuck greens all around wreath. Trim stems of paperwhite narcissus short; insert into water-filled vials. Tuck vials into wreath among greenery. Glue eggs into nest; let dry. Secure nest to wreath with pins. Occasionally spritz wreath with water to keep fresh-looking.

*N*othing says spring quite like daffodils, and this sunny square captures the season's mood as eloquently as Wordsworth's famous poem. Covered from corner to corner with the brightest of blooms, it will beam a friendly welcome from door or gate.

Daffy Dilly

You need:

floral foam in a square shape; dozens of different daffodils; small daisies (chamomile or feverfew are good choices); other small white flowers, such as snowdrops; yellow and white gingham wired ribbon

To do:

Thoroughly dampen foam form. Snip all flowers a couple of inches below their heads and place in water to keep as fresh as possible. Starting at left-hand corner, stick daffodil stems into foam, placing flowers closely together. Work around entire form until it is covered. Fill in any gaps with tiny clusters of daisies and a few of the other flowers. Mist with water. Finish off by tying ribbon into a big bow; affix to left corner with florist's wire and arrange ends to stream gracefully over wreath.

SUMMER

The great
William Shakespeare
wrote, "Summer's lease hath
all too short a date." Savor every single
moment with a wreath that shows
off the best of these
beloved months.

$\mathcal{B}$right, brilliant hues of orange and yellow mimic what some say is the most memorable time of day. Pay homage to the sun's daily descent with this dazzler.

Sunset Garden

You need:

bleached curly willow branches; muted green acrylic paint; cotton cloth; gloves; wire; clear glue; assorted flowers in shades of orange, yellow and red, such as ranunculus, sundrop, dill, zinnia and daisy; sprigs of similar leaves

To do:

To assemble sun-shaped base, soak willow branches in bathtub for 12–24 hours until pliable; they must be wet while you work with them. Cut three branches, each to the same measure as the desired circumference of center circle. Don gloves; apply 2 to 3 coats of paint diluted with water to all branches, spreading on with cloth and varying intensity for a more natural look. With paint still wet, bend and twist branches into a circle; secure with wire where needed. For rays, use thinner branches, leaving them in water until ready to use. To do, intertwine 2 or 3 thin branches, then bend and arrange into points as shown, weaving in and around circle and securing with wire. Repeat until you have formed 10 rays. If needed, touch up paint. Let branches dry completely, then glue down any stray pieces. Cut flower stems short and tuck in as desired. Add leaf sprigs. Mist with water.

So simple, so special—this blueberry-studded ring has a homespun touch, but it's so spare and serene, it could work in the most modern decor.

Berry Beautiful

You need:

grapevine wreath; yarrow; about a dozen pieces of any available vine; blueberries with foliage attached; pruners; clematis seed heads

To do:

Carefully trim yarrow stems and blueberry branches to appropriate lengths so you can tuck securely into grapevine wreath. Insert on either side of wreath as shown. Trim extra vine pieces to appropriate lengths and tuck vertically into right side of wreath to give a more casual effect. Add a few silky clematis seed pods on either side.

Traditional white roses, said to signify spiritual love and purity, teem forth from an atypical yet alluring oval shape. Such a bounty of blooms can't help but feel rich.

Rose Bowl

You need:

floral foam rectangle; kitchen or craft knife; thin wire; white roses; long strands of fresh or faux ivy; florist's pins; tassels (optional)

To do:

To make base, cut foam rectangle into an oval shape, sized as desired to fit door, window or wall. Thoroughly soak in water. Wrap wire around top of oval to form hanger in back. Cut stems of roses short and insert all over, completely covering foam form. When satisfied with the lushness of the wreath, string strands of ivy between roses, securing here and there with pins. Mist thoroughly with water. Use pins to secure tassels at top, if desired.

*T*he fiery color palette of this dazzler is ideal for summer but also hints at the coming autumn, providing a little preview of fall.

Red Square

You need:

12 red bamboo branches, all cut to 15-inch lengths; red raffia; hot-glue gun and glue sticks; sunflowers; zinnias; helenium; crocosmia; pruners

To do:

For each side, hot-glue three pieces of bamboo together to form one sturdy unit. Lash pieces with raffia at corners to form a square. Trim stems of blossoms as needed and tuck into raffia as shown. Mist with water.

*F*resh greenery, calla lilies and
lots of little waxflowers infuse a free-form
twig circle with the unique serenity of a
secluded glen you stumble upon by accident.

Feathered Flair

You need:

grapevine wreath; fresh calla lilies; waxflowers; ferns; clippers; floral vials (optional); thin vines or curly willow branches; long pheasant feathers

To do:

Trim flower stems as needed so you can tuck securely into wreath. Insert as desired until desired lushness is achieved. (If you wish to keep wreath fresh for longer period of time, tuck individual flowers into water-filled vials, then insert into wreath.) Add some thin twigs or curly willow vines here and there to give a wispier effect. Mist thoroughly with water. Finish by tucking feathers into grapevine.

On a steamy afternoon when it takes all the energy
you can muster just to make it to the hammock,
a display of daisies is as refreshing
as an out-of-the-blue breeze.

Daisy Dynamo

You need:

floral foam wreath; Shasta daisies; yellow daisies; feverfew; honeysuckle; yarrow; potato-vine berries; pruners; florist's wire

To do:

Thoroughly dampen foam form. Cut stems to appropriate length so you can poke into foam. Place flowers as desired, securing with florist's wire if needed. Add tiny bunches of berries here and there. Mist with water.

*I*magine coming upon an outdoor oasis that's green as far as the eye can see and you get the theme here. Lots of eucalyptus tucked in means an unforgettable aroma.

Green Scene

You need:

floral foam wreath; seasonal greens with varied shapes and textures, such as sprigs of eucalyptus, pachysandra and inkberry leaves (or leaves from any broad-leaf shrub)

To do:

Thoroughly dampen foam form. Starting in one spot and working around clockwise, insert greens, working in layers for a dense yet graceful look. Mist thoroughly with water.

This gorgeous gaggle of shells
has the power to transport you to the shore.
Close your eyes for a moment, take
a deep breath and listen—can you hear
the ocean in the distance?

Shore Thing

You need:

12-inch straw or plastic foam wreath; sufficient thin cloth (such as muslin or gauze) to cover wreath form; seashells in assorted sizes; dried starfish; hot-glue gun and glue sticks; grosgrain ribbon

To do:

Wrap wreath form completely with fabric, hot-gluing as necessary to hold in place. Hot-glue shells and starfish all over so fabric is hidden. Add a bow to top of finished wreath; hang with a length of ribbon.

RESOURCE GUIDE

*E*verything you need for making wreaths is widely available. Most art-supply or hobby shops, or even large discount stores with a crafts section, will have all the basic elements and then some. If you can't find exactly what you need locally, or just prefer the convenience of having supplies delivered directly to your door, here are some suggestions. In addition to a huge assortment of wreath forms and related items, many of the web sites listed below also offer project ideas and how-to's.

www.save-on-crafts.com
Specifically, the Floral Supplies category packs plenty of options at stock-up prices.

www.thewreathdepot.com
Try here for unusual bases, such as Indian Currant, Dogwood, Mountain Birch and Manzanita, that will make your projects even more unique. They also offer a large array of pre-made wreaths suitable for gift-giving.

www.joann.com
This well-regarded chain covers all the bases in terms of supplies.

www.afloral.com
Point-and-click for interesting picks such as florist-quality eucalyptus in several colors, bark-covered wire, dried citrus fruits, dune grass, galax leaves and preserved wheat.

www.crafta.com
Visit here for tons of faux leaves and flowers, if you wish to make everlasting wreaths.

www.michaels.com
The mighty crafts emporium's online arm boasts, in addition to supplies, an interactive wreath-making tutorial.

PHOTO CREDITS

Antonis Achilleos: cover, pp. 2, 34, 38, 39, 40, 41, 42, 43, 44, 45, 48, 49, 64, 72, 73, 84, 85, 116, 117

John Bessler: pp. 34, 36, 37, 46, 47, 52, 53, 54, 55, 58, 59, 60, 61, 62, 63

Susan Byrnes: cover, pp. 2, 11, 12, 14, 16, 17, 18, 19, 22, 23, 24, 25, 26, 27, 94, 95, 114, 115

Brian Hagiwara: pp. 90, 91, 102, 103

Michael Luppino: pp. 20, 21, 28, 29, 30, 31, 34, 56, 57, 64, 76, 77, 80, 81, 96, 97, 106, 122, 123

Steven Mays: pp. 82, 104, 105

Michael Pateman: pp. 50, 51, 66, 67

Steven Randazzo: pp. 112, 113

Alison Rosa: pp. 82, 86, 87, 88, 89

Mark Thomas: pp. 32, 33, 106, 108, 109

Richard Warren: cover, pp. 2, 64, 68, 69, 70, 71, 74, 75, 78, 79, 82, 92, 93, 106, 110, 111, 118, 119

Notes

Notes

Notes